Blurred Lines

Can You Open Your Mouth Please

Zynthia Howard

Dedication

This is dedicated to all those who always wonder why people would say, "You just don't know how to talk to people or why you didn't just tell me that." It's just a little miss understanding that's all. We are going tackle it though. Come on lets tackle this communication thang.

Zynthia Howard

Hellooo I Need To Talk To You

So often we hear the phrase, "We need to talk." Usually we think, "Uhoh what have I done, and do I really want to hear this." Be honest with yourself, you probably be thinking, "I could go the rest of my life without this conversation." You could, but will you have a healthy and honest relationship? No mam and no sir. So, let's face it, in order to have relationships that will last, we have to be able to talk to one another. There is no way around it.

Besides, what you don't say out of your mouth, will be expressed through other actions. For example, Meet Malik, He is a married man who does not like his wife cooking. It's not that she can't cook, he just doesn't like her seasoning.

Instead of him having a conversation with her, he buys food from fast food restaurants for himself or get plates from coworkers. Now if Malik would have a conversation with his wife, suggesting the seasoning he likes, the problem with the food would be solved. To every problem, there will be a solution found through a conversation. Being able to communicate well with others is a learned behavior. If you don't know how, you can learn. The million-dollar question is do you want to learn? How well do you receive change? Do you like change? I mean who does? Change can be scary, it's like your walking with blind folds on trying to go through a new house. In that house you don't know where the couch is sitting, you are praying that you don't trip and hurt yourself or even worse run slap into the wall head first.

What if you could think about change like driving that car that you look at every chance you get or the one you post on Facebook with the caption "Soon we will be together, driving through all kinds of weather". Change can be however you picture it. One thing for certain, you can never improve without change. So, let's put this, "I can't open my mouth and talk when I really need to because I never been able to", in a choke hold until it goes to sleep. Now that we got that out the way, lets uncover why you are sitting there with your lips pressed together, while in your mind saying all kinds of stuff that nobody hears but you and Jesus.

I mean that's cool if you are praying but right now we supposed to be talking. I'm asking you questions, *you just looking*, I'm making statements concerning us, *you just looking,* I get quiet, annnnd, *you just looking.* Who want to be talking to a human boomerang? Everybody want to and need to be heard. Just like the old school lyric, "It takes two to make a thing go right."

Why Don't You Just Say It!!

It can be extremely frustrating to people when they can see the wheels in your mind turning, yet nothing is coming out your mouth. I mean wrinkles come on your forehead and everything, still not a word. You even relax your brow and make the ooooh ok now I understand face expression, still not a word. It makes the person want to do you like a soda. You know when you shake a soda up, then open that top, and it just spills out? Yes, it makes the person want to shake the words out your mouth. They know they in there.

In order to effectively communicate with anybody, we must understand that everybody is not in the same place and you must meet people where they are. First you must understand why and where they are. Everything that you are stems from your childhood. Our childhood shapes the way we think as adults. For example, Meet Kisha, as a child she was mistreated by her siblings and sometimes her parents. Kisha never had an outlet to express the hurt she was enduring daily so she kept everything bottled up in the inside and learned to suppress it. Also, she never saw her parents talking to each other in a civil manner. They were always arguing and never coming to some type of agreement. The attitude was, "this is how I feel, and you need to go with it or leave." Kisha grew up not being able to talk to others about how she felt because she wasn't giving the opportunity to as a child and, she became afraid of confrontation as well due to seeing that her parents talk would turn into one.

Consequently, situations like Kisha's brings fear. This is the main factor that hinders you from opening your mouth. Fear of losing someone, saying the wrong thing, looking like the bad guy, receiving negative feedback, the picture it might portray, losing the upper hand, and being vulnerable.

To get rid of this fear mentality, you must acknowledge that it is there. Then you have trace where did it come from, dig its roots up and kick it out!!! There is no need for a thirty-day notice, serve fear an immediate eviction notice. Also, while you are kicking it out, send stubborn with him as well because he the one keeping your mouth close.

Fix Your Face

Have you ever witnessed a person walking passed you looking like they ready to fight the world? What did you do? Did you jump in front of them and say, Heyyyyy!!!! How are youuu!!! Ten times out of ten you moved out of their way and didn't say a word. Well, we can make people feel the same way about us.

Who is going to want to talk to you, when every time they try, you are sitting there with a stank face. I mean the whole time they are talking, you got one eyebrow up and wrinkles all in your face looking crazy. Would you want to talk to that face? Its distracting and it can make the other person irritated. Eventually the person will get mad, now both of you sitting there looking crazy. You must always be in a place mentally where you can be approached about any situation. Speaking of being approachable, don't automatically fold up your arms when somebody call your name. This is an unwelcoming look. If you haven't just finished break dancing, there is no reason for you to be in this stance.

Yesss, some conversations are going to make you feel some type of way. You must get past that feeling of offence because somebody coming to you about an issue that's about you. The whole time they talking you sitting there about to explode because you are thinking of all the issues that the other person has instead of trying to understand the issue from their point of view.

Calm down, relax, and release the tension out of your face. Understand if they didn't care about you, then this conversation would not be happening. Also realize this is not an attack on your character, it is simply pointing out where the two personalities clash and its time for a solution to come. Now you looking like a person who want to talk.

Woo!! Stop Looking At Me

Have you ever met a person that look you straight in your eyes every time you open your mouth to talk to them? How did that make you feel? Were you creeped out? Did it make you feel more comfortable? What did you see when you looked in their eyes? The eyes tell a story way better than the mouth ever could.

What you are saying out your mouth should line up with what's in your eyes. Usually your eyes will tell a more intense story that your mouth. Have you heard a person say, "They were talking to me with out even saying a word."? They are talking about the eyes. A person can detect when you have lost interest or didn't have any to begin with in the conversation. The eyes also can give a person a better understanding of what you are trying to say. You know sometimes we don't find the right words to get our point across. Its important to allow a person to see your eyes so that they can get a full understanding on what you are trying to say.

We can't talk about the eyes with out discussing the wandering eye. Your eyes should not be all over the place when you are in a conversation. Who wants to talk to somebody that has their eyes glued to the tv or got their head down texting while scrolling through social media? Do you enjoy having a discussion in public and the other person looking everywhere but at you? I mean they speaking to everybody they know and pointing at stuff interrupting your train of thought. You probably would just quit talking because the person is showing you that they are uninterested. Lets fixed our eyes on the other person in the conversation and give them our undivided attention.

You Didn't Hear A Word I Said

Alright let's get one thing straight, just because you hear me doesn't mean you were listening. You can let my voice go through your ears but immediately put up a stop sign when it tries to enter your mind.

For instance, can you imagine spending like an hour talking to somebody all about how you feel and when its their turn to talk its something completely opposite of what you were just saying? Their response has nothing to do with what you just talked about, its something completely different. You thinking to yourself, "Did they hear anything I just said".

This is so frustrating to anyone. You must learn how to listen no matter what is being said. You must clear your mind. You cannot go into a conversation with prepackage responses. You cannot treat conversations like the reject option on your phone with one of those prepared text messages.

You must walk into every conversation as if its your first day on a brand-new job. You know how it is on your first day of work right? You walk in not knowing what to expect. Everything somebody is saying, you are taking notes in your mind. Why would you do this? It's all because you want to respond with being the best employee in the place!! When they ask you something, you want to be able to just perform!!! You want to understand the job so strong that it takes everybody by surprise. This is the same way you need to approach a conversation.

You will find when you do this, your level of understanding will shoot up to the roof!!! You will start hearing people say, "I feel like you just get me", verses hearing, "I don't know why I even waste my breath talking to you."

Remember when it comes to listening, your ears are just the body guards, but the mind is the celebrity.

Excuse me, watch your mouth!!

How many people have you been overjoyed to talk to, when every time they opened their mouth it sounded like they had lost their mind? Their words are just awful. Every word they use is crazy offensive and so not necessary. Talking to them is like listening to a volcano erupt. You know people run from volcanos not to them.

When talking to someone, you must think about how you would want a person to talk to you. Would you want somebody to talk to you like you stole their money and ran over their childhood pet all in the same day? Ummm I think not.

If we could be honest, what you dish out is usually something that you can't even receive. You expect people to be able to handle what comes out of your mouth but if they talk like that to you, it's a whole different story. Now suddenly you ready to fight or flight. Listen you must talk to people as if you are talking to your most favorite person in the world. I'm not saying kiss up to them, but I am suggesting that you talk to them with respect no matter what the topic is.

Respect goes a long way in a conversation. You must learn how to express your emotions without coming unglued. You can be in total disagreement with someone and not talk sideways to them not one time during the conversation. Also, you must not take on the attitude, "OOOOh you want to feel this way about me, well guess what I'm about to hit you below the belt." Then you say something so hurtful and completely irrelevant to the conversation just, so you can feel like you have redeemed yourself. Understand when someone is coming to you about a issue at hand, it's not about who can be the biggest loser but how can we resolve this issue and the both of us be satisfied.

When talking to someone we must not lose the focus of even having the conversation. The focus should always be to get an understanding. When you get an understanding, it is followed with a solution. No understanding=no solution.

I Can't Deal With Your Tone!!

The Tone/attitude of a conversation can cause people to receive you or totally dismiss you. Picture you talking on the phone and in the middle of the conversation you hear a dial tone, are you going to keep talking? Ten times out of ten you will hang up. Why? Its because you heard the dial tone and you no longer heard the person on the other end. This is the same way it is when you are in the conversation. When the tone changes, you will no longer hear that person anymore, it just becomes noise loud in your ear. Who got time for that? Just like you will hang up the phone when you hear the dial tone, a person will hang up the conversation if the tone is not right. The tone is important. The tone of a conversation can make a person shut down and be done. You know people have this mentality, "I don't have to listen to this, especially when the tone is off the charts.

You must understand just because you don't like what's being said, doesn't mean you automatically begin a shouting match. If their voice is on five, then yours need to be on three. You always want to come a little lower than them so that there can be a balance. Also, if a person is already frustrated, if you get on their level with your tone will only add fuel to the fire.

Now let's not get it twisted, sometimes a cocktail can be used in a conversation. Your tone can be calm and collected but the words can be like venom. Just because your tone is cool doesn't mean your words should be like fire.

The tone should never be used to manipulate anyone. It should be at a level where both people can have a chance to understand and receive what is being said. Remember conversations is not to get you to do what I want, but to get a mutual understanding. It's not to make someone your puppet and the strings are being pulled with your tone.

My hope for you to be free from the things that has been keeping you from be effective communicator. May your perception about conversations be changed today. May you receive understanding like never before. May you be able to talk about things and come to a solution in a peaceful manner In Jesus name amen.

You can find me on social media under Zynthia Howard. I have a public page where I write poetry daily. Also I am on twitter, and Instagram.

Made in the USA
Columbia, SC
06 March 2024